Financial Markets

Money and Me

Financial Markets

by
Ray Sobczak

Rourke Publications, Inc.
Vero Beach, FL 32964

Photo on page 2 by Jim Whitmer.

Produced by Salem Press, Inc.

Copyright © 1997, by Rourke Publications, Inc.
All rights in this book are reserved. No part of this work may be used or reproduced in any manner whatsoever or transmitted in any form or by any means, electronic or mechanical, including photocopy, recording, or any information storage and retrieval system, without written permission from the copyright owner except in the case of brief quotations embodied in critical articles and reviews. For information address the publisher, Rourke Publications, Inc., P.O. Box 3328, Vero Beach, Florida 32964.

∞ The paper used in these volumes conforms to the American National Standard for Permanence of Paper for Printed Library Materials, Z39.48-1984.

Library of Congress Cataloging-in-Publication Data
Sobczak, Ray, 1936-
   Financial Markets / by Ray Sobczak.
      p.   cm. — (Money and me)
   Includes bibliographical references and index.
   Summary: A story about a young boy who wants to learn how to make the most of the money he is earning provides information about different kinds of investments.
   ISBN 0-86625-613-X
   1. Stocks—Juvenile literature. 2. Bonds—Juvenile literature. 3. Investments—Juvenile literature. 4. Financial instruments—Juvenile literature. 5. Money market—Juvenile literature. [1. Investments. 2. Stocks. 3. Bonds.] I. Title. II. Series.
HG4661.S634   1997
332.6—dc21   97-6364
                                                                                        CIP
                                                                                         AC

First Printing

PRINTED IN THE UNITED STATES OF AMERICA

Contents

Markets for Investments

Like many of his friends, David Andrews got a weekly allowance from his parents. Now that he was in the sixth grade, his allowance was not enough for everything he wanted, such as going out with his friends. He decided to earn some "extra" money. He put up a sign on the bulletin board of his apartment building, offering to do errands.

David used his bike to run the errands. The tires wore out, so he needed new ones to stay in business.

David's parents agreed to help him out by *investing* in his business, or providing money for it. They gave him money to buy bike tires. David promised to pay them back with money he earned.

After two months, David discovered that after paying all his expenses and paying back his parents, he still had $100 left in *profit*. He bought a set of basketball trading cards for $20 and decided to put the other $80 in the bank.

Investing the Profits

David asked his father to help him open a *bank account*. He knew that banks are safe places to save money. Bank accounts even pay *interest* as a way of getting people to save.

Children can begin to invest with money earned doing chores for other people.
(James L. Shaffer)

At the bank, David saw posters advertising *certificates of deposit* and *money market* accounts that paid interest rates higher than the 3 percent rate that his new savings account earned. David asked his father if he could get higher earnings from his savings. His father suggested, "Why don't we find out? Let's go to the meeting of the investment club that's being organized in our apartment building."

What Is Investing?

Later that week, Mr. Robinson, a financial planner, spoke at the investment club meeting. He began by describing what it meant to invest and some basic types of investments.

Investing means letting someone else use your money. The money might be used to run a business. David had used his parents' investment money for his business, to buy the bike tires he needed. Money from an investment also might be used to buy something, like a car or a house. Even the government uses other people's money.

Whoever borrows money from an investor promises to pay it back in some way. The investment might take the form of a *loan*. A bank account, for example, is a loan from an investor to a bank. Borrowers promise to pay back loans, with *interest*. Interest is a reward to the lender for

Computer entries have almost replaced printed stock certificates such as this. **(AP/Wide World Photo)**

TYPES OF FINANCIAL MARKETS	
• Stock markets	• Mutual funds
• Bond markets	• Commodity markets
Corporate	• Currency markets
Government	

making the loan. It usually is a percentage of the loan. Someone borrowing $1,000 for a year, for example, might promise to repay the $1,000 with 5 percent interest. He or she would pay a total of $1,050—the $1,000 of the loan plus $50 in interest.

Investors also might purchase a *share*, or part, of a business. Instead of getting a promise that their money will be paid back, they receive part of any profits that the business earns. Investors who want their original money back can sell the shares of the business (sometimes called *stocks*) to someone else.

Other investments involve neither a promise to repay nor a share in ownership of a business. Investors might simply buy something hoping that it will go up in price, so that they can resell it at a profit. This is called *speculation*.

Where Do People "Buy" Investments?

Mr. Robinson described the buying and selling of investments as taking place in *financial markets*. A financial market is like a store or a market. Rather than offering groceries or shoes, though, financial markets offer different ways to invest money. You might choose to make a loan, to buy a stock, or to *speculate* on some item. Markets exist for each of these types of investment.

Markets for Loans

When most people think of borrowing money, they think of going to a bank for a loan. Sometimes a borrower doesn't want to go to a bank. Maybe the bank charges too high a rate of interest. Maybe the loan is too big for the bank to make. The bank might even refuse to make the loan because it does not believe that the borrower can pay it back.

A business can borrow money by issuing, or selling, a *bond*. A bond is a written promise to pay back a loan, with interest. Businesses pay back loans from the money they earn selling products or services.

Governments also issue bonds. Governments, unlike businesses, do not sell products to try to make a profit. Their income comes mostly from taxes they collect. They use this income to pay back bonds.

Bond markets are where investors make loans to businesses and governments by buying bonds. Investors buy bonds to get the interest payments. They also get a promise that their investment will be returned on a certain date.

Someone who owns a bond might want to sell it now rather than wait until when the borrower has promised to pay back the investment. That person could make a second sale of the bond, to another investor. Sales such as these are made in *secondary markets*.

Stock Markets

Stock markets offer shares of ownership in businesses, called *stocks*. People who own them are called *shareholders* or *stockholders*. Businesses might need money to grow, to buy new machines, or to hire new workers. They can get that money by selling shares.

David remembered when he needed tires for his bike. Instead of borrowing money from his parents to buy the tires, he could have sold them shares in his business.

Shareholders get part of the profits that businesses earn. These shares of profits are called *dividends*. Usually, dividends are paid in cash.

Sometimes they are paid as additional shares in the company. When profits of a business improve, dividends become larger. That makes shares in the business worth more. Shareholders make money both from dividends and from increases in the value of shares.

Stocks also can go down in price, so people who buy them should realize that they *could* lose money.

Mutual Funds

It is risky to invest money in only one company. The company may not earn a profit and therefore may not be able to pay back a loan. It might not be able to pay dividends, and its stock price could fall. Investors then would lose money.

Investors can avoid this risk by buying shares in a mutual fund. A *mutual fund* is a collection of investments, usually stocks or bonds. When you buy a share in a mutual fund, you actually buy several different investments. A stock mutual fund, for example, might own dozens of different stocks.

The advantage of owning shares in a mutual fund is *diversification*, or having a variety of investments. If one investment doesn't earn money, the others might.

Funds have managers who are paid to select investments. Investors do not have to worry about picking individual investments. They just pick a mutual fund.

Commodity Markets

Sometimes investors want to invest in a product rather than in a business. This type of investing is called *speculating*. Investors buy a product and hope that it will go up in price. David hoped that his basketball trading cards would be worth more someday but hadn't realized that he was speculating.

Traders on the floor of the New York Mercantile Exchange, a commodities exchange, trade rapidly in response to news about the opening of an oil pipeline. (AP/Wide World Photos)

Investors can invest in different products in the *commodity markets*. Rather than buying and selling the actual products such as basketball cards, investors buy and sell *contracts*. These contracts are promises to deliver products at a certain price and on a certain date. If the price of the product goes up, the buyers of contracts make a profit because they own the right to buy the product at the old, lower price. They never actually have to buy the product. They can just sell the contracts back at the new, higher price.

Investors buy and sell contracts for such items as beef, eggs, oil, cotton, gold, and silver. They try to profit from *speculating*, or guessing the direction prices will move. Some sellers are not speculating. Farmers, for example, might want to guarantee what price they will receive for their products. They can sell contracts to guarantee a price.

Currency Markets

People sometimes need the *currency* (money) of another country. Tourists, for example, may need foreign currency when they travel. David still had a few *pesos* left from when his family visited Mexico.

Businesses may wish to buy products from someone in another country. They have to pay for the products with the currency of that country.

Currencies do not always have the same prices in relation to one another. A dollar might buy 100 Japanese yen one month and 105 yen the next month. It might buy 1.5 British pounds one month but only 1.4 pounds the next month. The prices depend on how much people want each currency. People might want more yen, for example, to buy more Japanese cars. They may also wish to invest in Japanese securities, such as stocks and bonds.

Where do people get foreign currency? Often, a bank can supply it. Where, though, do the banks get it?

In the *currency markets*, traders exchange one currency for another. Traders might be banks, businesses that need foreign currency, or *speculators*. Speculators in these markets are investors who buy currencies they think will go up in price.

CURRENCY EXCHANGE RATES (FEBRUARY 7, 1997)

Comparison	Rate	Percentage Change from Previous Week
Japanese yen to the U.S. dollar	122.60	+1.00
German marks to the U.S. dollar	1.6568	+1.12
Canadian dollars to the U.S. dollar	1.3495	+0.12
U.S. dollars to the British pound	1.6399	+2.44

How Do Financial Markets Work?

Ms. Barnes, from an investment firm, spoke at the next investment club meeting. She described how financial markets operate. She also explained how investors could learn more about different investments and how to select the best ones for themselves.

Financial markets can be complicated. Most investors get help from a *broker*, a professional who works in the financial markets. Brokers work for investment firms, which specialize in making investments.

Some financial markets, Ms. Barnes said, operate through financial centers, or *exchanges*, in major cities around the world. The *New York Stock Exchange* and the *Chicago Board of Trade* are two large U.S. exchanges.

Investment firms buy membership in an exchange. The exchange then allows them to make trades of investments through representatives of the exchange. These representatives are called *traders*, or sometimes *specialists*.

Traders gather around information screens at the New York Stock Exchange. (AP/Wide World Photos)

How Investments Reach the Markets

Ms. Barnes explained how investments become available to investors. The company selling the investment makes an *initial public offering* through an investment firm. This is the first time the investment is available to anyone. The investment firm then sells large quantities (blocks) of the investment to other firms, mutual funds, pension funds, and other large investors. These new owners then sell the investments through an exchange.

Most investors do not arrange their own trades. They trade through *brokers*, who are trained and licensed to arrange trades. The broker for a buyer contacts other brokers to find a client who wants to sell. The broker also might contact one of the exchange's traders or specialists.

Some trading is done in other ways. The *National Association of Securities Dealers* (NASD) uses a computer network to complete trades of stocks among brokers. It does not use a central exchange. Many corporations offer stock directly to investors. Small corporations may sell stock directly through brokerage firms. The most common way of buying stocks, though, is through a broker.

Mutual funds are traded directly through the businesses that run the funds. Brokerage businesses also trade in mutual funds for their customers.

Loans and Mortgages

Ms. Barnes then talked about loans and mortgages as other types of investments. Investors can make loans through the financial markets. These loans take the form of *bonds*.

The U.S. government sells bonds through banks and the Federal Reserve System, a set of banks that the U.S. government uses. Each month, the Federal Reserve System holds auctions for government *bonds*, *bills*, and *notes*. All three are referred to in general terms as bonds. They differ only in their *maturity*, or the length of the loan. Each represents money owed by the federal

Savings bonds, which are sold at banks, provide a way to invest in the government without using a broker.
(James L. Shaffer)

government, money that the government promises to repay with interest. Investment firms buy most of these bonds and then sell them to clients. Individual investors also can buy these bonds at the auctions.

Investors also can buy other bonds from the federal government. Some government bonds represent different collections of *mortgages*. A mortgage is a loan taken out to buy real estate — land or buildings. Some government agencies make mortgage loans to people to buy houses, and to businesses to buy buildings. The agencies then put several loans together in a *fund* and sell bonds representing shares in the fund. That way, they get money to make even more mortgage loans. Bonds of each fund are sold through the financial markets. An investor who buys a bond from one of these funds is *indirectly* lending money to someone who buys real estate. The government guarantees payment of the bonds.

State, city, and other local governments also sell bonds. These are called *municipal bonds*. The money from these bonds might be used to build hospitals, roads, or schools. The government that issues the bond promises that it will be repaid.

Many bonds are sold by businesses. The businesses might use the money to buy buildings or machines, or to hire new workers. When a business issues a bond, it is the only one guaranteeing that the bond will be paid back. That makes business, or *corporate*, bonds less safe as investments than government bonds, which are guaranteed by the government. Because of this higher risk, corporate bonds usually pay a higher rate of interest.

Currency Markets

Investors can speculate on the prices of different currencies through the currency markets. *Currency markets* work through banks that keep foreign

Some businesses specialize in trading currencies for the public. (AP/Wide World Photos)

currencies available for customers and have deposits from foreign governments and businesses. People and businesses go to these banks to get the foreign currency they need to buy things in other countries.

Currencies trade through *contracts* similar to those in the commodities markets. By buying or selling a contract, an investor can try to profit from *speculation* about whether a currency will become more or less valuable. Businesses also can guarantee the price of a currency that they will need sometime later.

Reading About Investments

David wanted to learn about all the numbers he saw in the business pages of the newspaper. The night after the meeting, David and his father looked at the business page of the newspaper together.

David saw that each section of investment listings showed some of the same information. Each identified the item by name, such as the name of a stock or mutual fund. Each also had a price. Some of the listings showed a *rate of return*, or the percentage of the investment paid back each year (as interest on a bond or as dividends on a stock or mutual fund). The stock listings showed the high and low prices for the day. The change in price from the previous day also appeared.

Treasury bonds showed an interest rate, as well as the date of *maturity*. That is when investors would get back their original investment. David noticed that the prices for Treasury securities had decimals. His father explained that the "decimals" really were fractions representing 32nds of a dollar (about 3 cents). A price of 99.11 was $99 11/32, or about $99.34.

STOCK QUOTATIONS

52-Week High	Low	Stock	Dividend	Yield %	P/E	Sales 100s	High	Low	Close	Change
45½	37¼	Blue Chip Corp.	1.00	2.5	20	1200	40¼	39¾	40	+⅛
52	48½	Blue Flash Power	3.60	7.2	15	800	50⅝	49½	50	−⅛

52-Week High and Low: Tell the stock's highest and lowest prices during the past year. Stock prices are shown in dollar amounts and fractions of a dollar.

Stock: The name of the stock, often abbreviated.

Dividend: Dividends paid per share during the last year, in dollars. Blue Flash Power paid $3.60 in dividends for each share.

Yield %: The ratio of the annual dividend to the closing price, shown as a percentage.

P/E: Short for the price/earnings ratio. A ratio of the price of the stock to the company's earnings during the last year. The company's earnings are not shown in the stock quotations.

Sales 100s: Number of shares bought and sold that day. Most trades are multiples of one hundred shares, so sales are expressed in hundreds of shares.

High: Highest price paid for a share during the day.

Low: Lowest price paid for a share during the day.

Close: Price paid for a share in the last trade of the day.

Change: Difference between the closing price today and the closing price on the previous day of trading.

David's father said that many business magazines, newsletters, and investor services print information about investments. In addition, services such as Morningstar, Dunn and Bradstreet, Value Line, and Standard and Poor's print histories of price changes and returns, or *yields*, so that investors can see how a stock has performed over time. The yield on an investment, also called the *rate of return*, is the amount of money an investor gets back as dividends or interest. It is a percentage of the value of the investment.

Different *ratings services* compare investments on such factors as safety and the likelihood of a price increase. An increase in the price of an investment is called a *capital gain*. Investors use

---

MUTUAL FUND QUOTATIONS

Fund	NAV	Change	3 Year Return	1 Year Return
Intgrty Funds				
Climber	8.52	+0.01	10.4	15.1
Nester n	9.31	−0.07	7.2	8.3
Saver	11.23	+0.18	6.5	5.3

Fund: The name of the fund, sometimes abbreviated. "Intgrty Funds" is short for "Integrity Funds." Names of groups of funds sold by the same company usually appear in bold type. The funds within the group appear below the group name.

n: An "n" after a fund name means that it is a no-load fund. There is no charge to buy shares in the fund. Some funds have charges.

NAV: Net asset value, shown in dollars. The value of one share, calculated using the number of shares and the value of all assets (money and securities the fund owns). Shares are sold at the net asset value plus any sales charge. Shares are redeemed (bought back from investors) at net asset value minus any redemption charges.

Change: Change in net asset value from the previous day's trading. The Climber fund rose in price by 1 cent.

3 Year Return and 1 Year Return: The total return, shown as an annual percentage rate. The Nester fund increased in value by 8.3 percent during the last year and by an average of 7.2 percent during the previous three years.

TREASURY SECURITY QUOTATIONS (FEBRUARY 10, 1997)

Rate	Maturity	Bid	Yield	Bid Change
8.50	Jul 97	101.10	4.99	–0.01
5.50	Jul 97	100.03	5.01	.....
5.88	Nov 99	99.24	5.94	.....
7.88	Nov 99	104.25	5.91	.....

Rate: The interest rate stated on the security. The government makes interest payments based on the face value of the security and the stated interest rate.

Maturity: The date when the principal will be repaid.

Bid: The price offered for a security with face value of $100. The bid is expressed in dollars for the whole numbers. The numbers behind the decimal points represents 32nds of a dollar. The July, 1997, security with an interest rate of 8.50 percent costs $110 10/32, or $110.3125.

Yield: The value of interest payments divided by the current value of the security, expressed as an annual percentage rate. Securities priced over 100 will have a yield less than the rate in the first column.

Bid Change: The change in the bid price from the previous day's trading, expressed in dollars and 32nds of a dollar.

the information from these ratings services to make better investment choices.

Investment Strategies

The next investment club meeting focused on investment strategies. Everyone wants to make more money, but investors differ in how much risk they are willing to take. Some investors want to protect their *principal*, or the original amount invested. They do not want to risk losing any of their investment. Other investors might be willing to take some risk if they are rewarded for it. They can choose investments that change in value but might have higher yields.

David learned about the *risk/return tradeoff*. To earn higher returns, investors usually have to take more risks. *Diversification*, or buying different types of investments, can lessen risks.

One club member brought an investment pyramid diagram showing some different types

THE INVESTMENT PYRAMID

Options	
Commodities	
Gold, Silver and Diamonds	Art and Collectibles
Undeveloped Land	Oil and Gas Exploration
Income Real Estate	Leveraged Mutual Funds
Preferred or Common Stocks	Growth and Income Mutual Funds
Investment Grade Bonds	Balanced Mutual Funds
Variable Annuities and Life Insurance	Growth Stocks and Mutual Funds
Municipal Bonds and Zero Coupon Bonds	Home Ownership
Employment Investment Plans	Individual Retirement Accounts
Insured Certificates of Deposit	U.S. Treasury Bills, Notes, and Bonds
Savings and Checking Accounts (insured and interest-bearing)	U.S. Savings Bonds

of investments. The safest investments, with the lowest expected returns, were at the bottom. They represent a solid, safe base. The investments higher on the pyramid have higher returns but more risk. They should be a smaller part of most investors' portfolios.

CHAPTER 3

Who Does What?

Ms. Barnes had invited anyone interested to visit the investment firm where she worked. David got a day off from school for teacher meetings. He decided to take advantage of her offer. He wanted to find out about all the people who work at an investment firm and what happens there.

Ms. Barnes invited David into her office to talk. She explained that she is a *full-service broker* for her investment firm. That means she learned about different types of investments and had to pass tests about what she learned. With so many types of investments and laws concerning them, there is a lot to know.

Brokers are the most noticeable workers at investment firms. Most of an investor's contact with the firm is through a broker.

How People Become Investors

Ms. Barnes refers to people who invest with her help as *clients*. They come to Ms. Barnes from different places. Some are from clubs like David's. Current clients sometimes recommend Ms. Barnes to their friends. Sometimes people simply call the office looking for a broker.

When Ms. Barnes first meets with a client, they discuss services she can offer. They also discuss the client's goals in investing. If the client wishes to open an *investment account*, she helps the client to complete an application. They sign an agreement about the services she and her firm will provide. The client then opens the account by providing money. The money might come from a check, as a transfer from a bank account, or perhaps from an investment account with another firm.

Services a Broker Provides

As a broker, Ms. Barnes provides a variety of services. She tells her clients about the different investments her firm can sell. She also gives clients printed information about particular stocks, bonds, mutual funds, or other investments. She may give advice based on the goals the client told her about.

When clients buy or sell investments, they might pay a *commission* to Ms. Barnes. This is a payment for her services.

Investors who already know a lot about investing may not want to pay for as many services. They choose *discount brokerages*, which do not offer advice or information but have lower commissions.

Charles Schwab pioneered the idea of the discount brokerage. (AP/Wide World Photos)

CHARLES SCHWAB

Charles Schwab's ideas avoid the traditional approach of having brokers act as salespeople. In the old approach, brokers earn commissions by calling customers to offer advice and research on investments their firms are trying to sell.

Instead, Schwab's brokerage firm offers to trade stocks at low commissions. His brokers do not offer advice on stocks. The firm also sells mutual funds at no commission and with no transaction fees. It keeps fees and charges on other investments as low as possible. It even offers computer software that allows clients to trade using their own personal computers.

Other innovations include communicating with active investors by telephone, fax, or pager so that they have the latest information. Schwab's firm also offers plans to reinvest dividends automatically, with no fee.

Schwab uses technology and innovative methods. He also believes that investors should be able to meet the people who handle their investments. The firm has more than 200 branch offices all over the United States. The large number of branches means that many investors have a local branch that they can visit.

Investors like Schwab's approach. Between 1988 and 1994, the number of accounts rose from about 1 million to about 3 million. The value of those accounts rose from about $25 billion to about $120 billion.

How Clients Make Trades

Ms. Barnes explained what happens when a client decides to buy or sell an investment. As a broker, she acts as the client's *agent*, doing what the client wants and finding the best deal. She can find the most recent price for the investment on her computer, which is connected to various markets. She also can telephone a *market specialist* or *investment dealer* who works with a certain investment. That person can arrange the purchase or sale.

The client might decide to make the trade at the current price in the market. Instead, he or she might specify a price and wait until someone else is willing to make the other half of the trade. An investor may not be in a hurry to sell. He or she could ask for a high price and wait for a buyer willing to pay it.

Brokers stay in communication with their customers and the markets using telephones and computers— sometimes several at once. (Ray Sobczak)

Once she arranges a trade, Ms. Barnes confirms it with the investor. This usually happens by telephone. She can complete a trade for an investment that trades often, such as a stock, within a few minutes. Some investments do not trade as frequently. Matching a buyer and a seller can take longer for those investments.

Ms. Barnes sends information about each trade to *data processing workers* at her firm. These workers record the information in the client's account. They also send a written *confirmation* of the trade to the client. The confirmation tells the client the price at which the trade took place. It also tells the date the trade happened and lists any fees or commissions charged.

Ms. Barnes's firm sends its clients a *statement of account* once a month. The statement shows the investments the client owns, earnings from investments during the month, money received from selling investments, and money paid for investments. It also shows the value of each investment, on the date the statement was prepared. Those values change all the time. Some of Ms. Barnes's clients want information about their investments in between statements. They can telephone her or find the information in business newspapers and magazines.

David asked about other jobs related to investing. Ms. Barnes told him about some of those jobs.

Specialists

Trading specialists at financial exchanges help to arrange trades in particular investments. They focus on one or a few investments.

Some specialists and traders work in the bond markets. They may specialize in U.S. Treasury securities or in the *municipal bonds* issued by local, county, or state governments.

Mutual fund managers keep investors' money invested in the financial markets. They keep track of how much money comes into their funds, from new investments and as income from existing investments. They decide which particular investments to buy.

Some specialists develop computer programs that predict the best times to buy or sell investments.

SAM ZELL

Sam Zell has made a fortune by looking for value in businesses and real estate. He looks for companies that are inexpensive compared to what he thinks they are worth. His business empire includes industrial and service companies, large real estate partnerships and trusts, and a huge fund of money that he uses to buy companies. His holdings earned more than $17 million in 1994.

Some mutual funds copy his holdings. This allows investors to participate in his investment strategy. Not all of his investments have been profitable, so the funds do not always earn profits.

Zell enjoys his roles as a speculative developer of real estate and as a specialist in buying companies that he thinks are inexpensive. He admits that his success has created some problems. He says it is difficult for one man to control a large financial empire with many different locations and operations.

These specialists include *program technicians, market analysts,* and *economists.* Every day, trades based on computer programs, called *program trades,* add up to millions of dollars.

Predicting the Markets

Investors want to know if businesses are going to earn a profit, because that affects stock prices. Market analysts predict how much businesses will earn. They use information provided by businesses and governments. *Accountants* review the assets, debts, income, and expenses of businesses. This information also helps in predicting future earnings and profits.

Economists try to figure out how all the numbers in the economy fit together. They look at such things as interest rates, unemployment rates, and prices. They see how these numbers have changed in the past and predict changes in the future. Sometimes they predict what will happen if something else happens. For example, an economist might learn about a new tax law. The economist would use knowledge about how the economy works to predict how the law will affect stock prices.

Financial planners help investors decide how to achieve certain financial goals. Planners may work with investment firms. They suggest ways to use the investments that those firms sell. Independent planners do not work with any one investment firm. They help investors find good investments, then find out who sells them.

Who Provides the News?

Communications media are important to financial markets. Such large publications as *The Wall Street Journal* newspaper and *Barron's* magazine print information about daily news in the financial markets. Smaller investment magazines and newsletters print some of the same information.

The Wall Street Journal *provides business news from around the world.* **(Ben Klaffke)**

They might focus on particular types of investments. Local newspapers summarize business activity and markets in their business sections.

Television also provides news about financial markets. Ms. Barnes mentioned two particular shows on public television. *The Nightly Business Report* provides financial information, and *Wall Street Week* analyzes the markets. Cable television offers channels specializing in financial news. Some shows have guests who discuss the financial markets.

Perhaps the most-watched news from the financial markets is the *Dow Jones Industrial Average*. It is an average of the prices of the stocks of thirty large corporations listed on the New York Stock Exchange. Each major stock exchange has a similar number telling the value of the stocks traded on that exchange. When these numbers rise, investors on average make profits on their investments.

Some businesses specialize in rating investments. Their ratings predict earnings and evaluate safety. Standard and Poor's, Moody's, and Morningstar all provide ratings of stocks and bonds.

THE DOW INDUSTRIALS

The share prices of the thirty companies listed below are used to calculate the Dow Jones Industrial Average.

AlliedSignal, Incorporated
Alcoa
American Express Company
American Telephone & Telegraph
Boeing Company
Caterpillar Incorporated
Chevron Corporation
Coca-Cola Company
Walt Disney Company
Du Pont Company
Eastman Kodak Company
Exxon Corporation
General Electric Company
General Motors Corporation
Goodyear Tire and Rubber
    Company

Hewlett-Packard Company
IBM Corporation
International Paper Company
Johnson & Johnson
McDonald's Corporation
Merck & Company
3M Company
J. P. Morgan and Company
Philip Morris Companies
Procter & Gamble Company
Sears, Roebuck and Company
Travelers Group
Union Carbide Corporation
United Technologies
    Corporation
Wal-Mart Stores, Incorporated

Government agencies provide information on recent monthly economic statistics, such as unemployment, interest rates, and prices. Market analysts and economists use this information in their predictions.

All sorts of news affects financial markets. Weather, military operations, changes in governments and laws, medical news, and new products all can have effects on financial markets. Investment analysts follow news developments and predict effects of news on the markets.

Many people are involved in the financial markets, from traders to analysts to people who provide information. David wondered if he would ever know enough about the markets to have one of those jobs. Ms. Barnes said he was getting an early start.

CHAPTER 4

What Are the Rules?

The members of David's investment club wanted to what laws and rules would protect their investments. They also wanted to know their responsibilities as investors. One club member was a lawyer. At one meeting, he described the rules for businesses and investors in the financial markets.

The lawyer explained that international, national, state, and local governments have laws concerning financial markets. Various agencies are responsible for enforcing these rules.

The Securities and Exchange Commission

The *Securities and Exchange Commission* (SEC) is one such agency. Businesses that want to sell securities in the major U.S. financial markets must get permission from the SEC. They must give the SEC information about their financial condition and about the securities they intend to sell. The SEC decides if the investment meets federal requirements that protect investors.

Another important task of the SEC is to watch the financial markets and look for problems. People working for the SEC investigate complaints. They also look at how brokers and traders do business to make sure it is legal. They also may look at

Michael R. Milken was convicted of making illegal trades in the markets for high-yield "junk bonds."
(AP/Wide World Photos)

businesses listed on the exchange, the financial firms operating the exchange, or investors. People who break rules or laws may have to pay fines. They may even end up in prison.

The *North American Securities Administrators Association* acts like the SEC. It enforces securities laws and protects the public. It operates in the United States, Canada, and Mexico.

Making the Rules

Organizations in the financial markets make rules that businesses and traders must follow. They also provide ways for investors to get information about exchange members, especially brokers. Investors can find out about particular brokers from these organizations' files of past complaints.

The *Securities Investor Protection Corporation* provides insurance on investment accounts. Investment firms pay for this insurance. The insurance pays investors for losses that result from financial failures (bankruptcies) of member brokers or dealers.

The *Commodities Futures Trading Commission* sets rules for firms that trade in commodities. It checks that traders hold the proper licenses. It also keeps records of complaints related to commodities firms and brokers.

Brokers

Brokers in the financial markets must have a *license* to sell certain investments. To get a license, they have to learn about investments and laws. They must then pass tests about this information. Many investments can be sold only by someone with a license. Investors can be sure that licensed brokers know what they are doing.

When an investor opens an account with a brokerage firm, he or she signs an agreement stating the rules that the firm will follow. It also states rules that the investor will follow.

The brokerage firm agrees to act as an *agent* for the investor in making investments. That means that the firm will do what the investor wants. The investor selects the type of investments and the

Legal contracts set the rules for dealings between brokers and their clients. (Jim Whitmer)

level of risk desired. The brokerage firm then recommends certain investments. The firm agrees to make any trades requested by the investor. The firm agrees to confirm each trade.

Investors may decide to keep their stock and bond certificates at the brokerage firm. Doing this helps protect them from theft. Many stocks and bonds do not have paper certificates anymore. Ownership is recorded only as a computer entry.

A brokerage firm must send statements of account to investors at regular intervals. Most firms send statements monthly. The statements show the approximate value of investments. They also show the income received and expenses paid by the investor. Finally, they show the values of any trades. Investors are responsible for reporting any errors in their statements so mistakes can be corrected.

The brokerage firm must provide information about investors' accounts to the federal government. Investors pay taxes on investment earnings, so the government needs to know when investors make a profit.

Investors are responsible for paying for any investments within a short time. Usually this is three days or less. Investors who cannot pay for their investments must arrange for a loan. Loans from brokerage firms to investors are called *margin* arrangements.

What About Disagreements?

Sometimes investors and brokerage firms disagree about a trade. An investor might claim that a commission was higher than agreed. Perhaps an investor thinks that the brokerage did not get the best price for an investment. The contract between an investor and a brokerage firm usually states how disagreements will be settled.

Most often, investors and brokerage firms agree to *arbitration*. An arbitrator is someone impartial who will not benefit no matter who wins the dispute. The arbitrator decides who was right and if any money has to be paid by whoever was wrong.

Investors count on brokerage firms to do exactly what they are told. Sometimes firms take actions without asking the investor. If those actions result in a financial loss, the brokerage firm or the individual broker must pay that loss.

Trading in financial markets involves trust between brokerage firms and investors. Investors must choose a broker carefully. They should find out the reputation of the brokerage firm. The firm and its brokers should be licensed. Government and business agencies can help provide this information.

What Are the Risks and Benefits?

A lively discussion about the risks and benefits of investing took place at the investment club's next meeting. Mr. Stilson pointed out that investors can increase their wealth from *capital gains* (the value of an investment rising), *interest*, or *dividends*. Any investment, however, involves the risk of a loss of money. Mr. Stilson seemed to know a lot about these risks. He told the other club members about them.

Types of Risk

Risks include those from inflation, deflation, interest rates, particular businesses or markets, illiquidity, currencies, and changes in laws. *Inflation* means that a dollar will buy fewer goods now than it did earlier. In other words, prices have gone up. Any *principal* (money originally invested) that is returned is worth less than when it was invested. *Deflation risk* is the chance that the price of a company's product will fall. That could lower the price of the company's stock.

Changes in *interest rates* present other risks. If interest rates rise, bond prices tend to fall. That is because they pay the old, low interest on their principal. New bonds would pay the higher rate of interest, and a high rate of interest is worth more than a low rate. In addition, if interest rates fall, bond issuers may choose to pay them off early. (This is called *calling* a bond.) The investor then has to find some other investment to buy. If bond issuers still need money, they borrow it at the new, lower interest rates.

An investor runs the risk that a business's product will become unpopular. This is a type of *business risk.* Another type of business risk is that the company will be managed poorly and not earn profits. Investors can reduce these risks by investing in large, well-known, and stable companies. The stocks of these companies are known as *blue chip stocks.*

Market risk comes from changes in the overall market for a product. If a type of product becomes unpopular, the stock prices of all companies selling that product will tend to fall. Market risk can extend to the market as a whole—all stock prices may rise or fall together. When most investors expect stock prices to rise, it is called a *bull* market. When they expect stock prices to fall, it is called a *bear* market.

When businesses go "out of business," investors can lose their money.
(James L. Shaffer)

Illiquidity risk refers to the difficulty of selling an investment quickly. (Liquidity refers to money "flowing," so an "illiquid" investment is one that doesn't "flow" easily from one investor to another.) An investor who wants to sell right now may have to take a low price. Others may wait to find a buyer willing to pay a reasonable price. While they wait, the price may fall, or the investor may miss other investment opportunities.

Currencies change in value relative to one another all the time. This can cause profits or losses for investors. If the dollar falls in value against the German mark, for example, the stock prices of American companies tend to fall. At the same time, the prices of German companies tend to rise. U.S. bonds also would fall in value because the dollars that they represent have fallen in value.

Finally, changes in laws and rules can affect the value of investments. Tax laws, laws affecting trade, tariffs and quotas, and various rules all affect investments.

Costs of Investing

Mrs. Jones jumped in and said that there were known costs of investing, in addition to risks. She pointed out that investors often must pay commissions, annual fees to keep accounts, and charges for financial services. Such costs could wipe out the profit made on an investment.

Taxes also reduce earnings. If an investment rises in value, it is said to have a *capital gain*. Capital gains are taxed. So are dividends and interest.

Mr. Stilson said that tax laws allow for *exemptions* on some investment income, meaning that the income is not taxed. Interest on U.S. government bonds is not taxed by states. Interest on municipal bonds is not taxed by the federal government. Investors also can protect against taxation by

Investment income must be reported on state and federal tax returns. (Jim Whitmer)

putting money into *tax-deferred* accounts. One example is an *Individual Retirement Account*. No taxes need to be paid on those accounts until money is withdrawn from them.

Why Bother Investing?

With all the risks and costs of investing, Mrs. Jones asked, why does anyone bother? Mr. Stilson answered quickly. Financial costs and risks exist even for people who do not invest. Having money in your wallet, for example, exposes you to inflation risk. Investing, though, offers the possibility of financial rewards in addition to the risks. Many of the risks can be lessened, too.

Some investments, for example, guarantee the return of principal. These include accounts in insured banks, savings and loans, and credit unions. The federal government promises to pay all principal and interest on U.S. bonds. Some municipal bonds also offer protection of principal. Rating services predict the safety of other bonds, so investors can buy the safest ones.

Investors must be careful about market risk with stocks. Stocks tends to have more changes in price (called *volatility*) than other investments over short periods of time. Over long periods of time, however, stocks tend to have a higher total return. The history of a company and its stock is important. A stock is less risky if it has paid dividends consistently. Consistent earnings by the company from year to year also signal less risk.

Mr. Stilson added that investing is important for the economy as a whole. Businesses get money to operate or expand. The businesses then provide jobs for workers. Governments pay for services they provide by selling bonds, as well as through taxes. The currency exchanges make international trade much easier.

Which Risks to Take

All financial choices involve risk. The question is which types of risk an investor is willing to take. Young investors with immediate needs, such as for college tuition, should make sure that they will have money right when they need it. They should avoid illiquidity risk. They can take some other risks, such as from volatility, with money they don't need right away. They have long lives ahead of them, and any losses from volatility now can be made up later.

Older people usually avoid market risk and investments with high volatility. They depend on their investments to provide a steady income used to pay living expenses.

Making a Plan

David's father spoke up. He said that different investors have different plans for investment. David is investing to pay for a college education. Other investors might be saving for retirement. Whatever goals an investor has, the investment plan should match them.

It is important to make plans early. An early start in investing can make a big difference. A small difference in interest rates can make a big difference in earnings, too. Mr. Stilson had a chart showing an example.

VALUE OF A $1,000 INVESTMENT		
Years	Return on Investment (compounded annually)	
	5%	10%
0	$1,000	$1,000
10	1,629	2,594
20	2,653	6,727
30	4,322	17,449
40	7,040	45,259

At a 5 percent rate of return, an investor would have more than seven times the original investment at the end of forty years. At a 10 percent rate of return, the investor would have more than forty-five times the original investment. Even though the rate of return was only twice as high, the value of the investment would be more than six times as high.

This is an example of *compounding*, or earning returns on the returns from previous years. In the first year, $1,000 invested at a 5 percent return would earn $50. The investor would have $1,050 at the end of the year. In the second year, the investor would earn another $50 on the $1,000 principal. In addition, the $50 earned the previous year would earn $2.50. The total return for the second year would be $52.50. The investor would have $1,050 + $52.50 = $1,102.50.

The $2.50 earned from compounding might not seem like much, but compounding adds up over time. With compounding, $1,000 turns into $45,259 in 40 years with a 10 percent rate of return. Without compounding, it would be only $5,000.

Beginning to Invest

The investment club members planned for the next meeting. At that meeting, they would each decide how much to invest to start. They would choose an investment firm and set the rules for the club. They would pick people to do more research on investments they thought they might buy.

After the meeting, David talked with his father about starting his own investment plan. They

Even youngsters can form investment plans. (James L. Shaffer)

decided to put some of David's money into the
investment club. David wanted to open his own
brokerage account, but only adults can do that.
His father agreed to open a *custodial account* for
him with a local brokerage firm. The custodial
account would have David's name on it.

David thought that a money market mutual
fund would be a good way to start. It would
give some diversity and allow small additions
to his investments. He planned to study other
investments so he could diversify as his investments
grew. He looked forward to learning more from
the other members of the investment club. He
especially looked forward to watching his
investments grow.

*An investment plan
and wise investing
can help in achieving
financial goals.
(James L. Shaffer)*

Glossary

bear: Someone who believes that a market will fall in value. A market expected to fall in value is called a bear market.

blue chip stock: Stock in a company known for the quality of its products and for its ability to pay dividends. Blue chip stocks are relatively safe investments.

bull: Someone who believes that a market will rise in value. A market expected to rise in value is called a bull market.

call: Repayment of a bond before its maturity date. Borrowers might call bonds if interest rates fall.

capital gain: An increase in the value of an investment. A decrease in value is a capital loss.

custodial account: An account opened for one person by another. Children cannot legally take some responsibilities. Because of this, adults may have to open custodial accounts for them. The adults take the responsibilities.

diversification: Owning different types of investments. Diversification reduces certain risks of investing.

dividend: A payment to a stockholder in a company. It comes from the company's earnings. Most often, dividends are paid in cash. Sometimes a dividend is paid as additional shares in the company.

interest: Money paid to lenders. Payment of interest encourages lenders to make loans.

maturity: The date of maturity on a bond is when the borrower promises to pay back the investor's money.

money market: The market for short-term loans. Money market accounts allow investors to buy shares in diversified packages of short-term loans.

mortgage: An agreement for a loan. Money from the loan is used to buy real estate.

mutual fund: A business that takes investors' money and buys a variety of investments. Mutual funds help investors to diversify.

principal: The original amount of an investment.

real estate: Buildings and land.

stock: A share in ownership in a company.

yield: The amount of interest or dividend on an investment divided by the value of the investment. The yield is expressed as a percentage.

Sources

Books

Ady, Ronald W. *The Investment Evaluator.* Englewood Cliffs, N.J.: Prentice-Hall, 1984. Provides brief information for making investment choices.

The Consumer Reports Money Book. Yonkers, N.Y.: Consumer Reports Books, 1992. Describes how different investment choices can meet consumer needs, goals, and finances.

The Council of Better Business Bureaus. *Investor Alert!* Elmsford, N.Y.: The Benjamin Company, 1988. Describes various frauds against investors and how to avoid them.

Crittenden, Alan. *The Almanac of Investments.* Novato, Calif.: Crittenden Books, 1984. Interesting examples of different types of investments.

Dolan, Ken, and Darla Dolan. *Straight Talk on Money.* New York: Simon and Schuster, 1993. Practical and easy to understand.

Dow Jones-Irwin Business and Investment Almanac. Homewood, Ill.: Business One Irwin, annual. Includes statistics on various types of investments for several decades. Contains yields on stocks.

Gardner, David, and Tom Gardner. *The Motley Fool Investment Guide.* New York: Simon and Schuster, 1996. Presents an up-to-date, no-nonsense approach to investing.

Nichols, Donald R. *Starting Small, Investing Smart.* Homewood, Ill.: Dow Jones-Irwin, 1984. Lists ways of investing small amounts of money.

Porter, Sylvia. *Your Own Money.* New York: Avon Books, 1983. Has chapters on investing aimed at young people.

Other Sources

CNBC: A cable television channel providing business and financial information.

Money: A magazine that reviews investments and provides tips on investing.

Nightly Business Report: A public television show giving each day's business news.

The Wall Street Journal: A daily newspaper (weekdays) focusing on business news.

Wall Street Week: A public television show providing investment information and suggestions.

Index